The Moment of Capture

The Moment of Capture

John Lambremont Sr.

Copyright © 2017 John Lambremont Sr.

All rights reserved

ISBN: 978-1-943170-23-4

Cover Image: John Lambremont Sr.

Cover and Interior Design: Jane L. Carman

Published by: Lit Fest Press, Carman, 688 Knox Road 900 North, Gilson, Illinois 61436

Outside the box

This book is dedicated to my father-in-law and mother-in-law, now deceased, Trung Han Hau and Hoa Thi Phan, whose photo graces this volume's cover.

TABLE OF CONTENTS

Preface	1
The Age-Old Struggle	3
The Paranormals	6
The Day Our Home Exploded	7
One Southern Saturday	9
Corn	12
Feliz Año Nuevo	13
Suburb in Rondo	15
Delta Deep Freeze	18
Small Favor	19
Ulinary Uprising	22
Rapture	24
The Totality of Circumstances	25
Screech	27
A Sequence	28
Foreign Beyond	29
Fun with Shorty and Rondo	31
Abasement	32
In the Interim	34
Separate Classes	36
Food Fight	38
I, Drunkie	39
Slipping Gears	41
In the Aftermath	42
The Masher and the Maiden	43
Pachuco Y Juanito	44
Earth Invader	46

Dummy	47
The Gift	50
Batter-Whipped	51
Ultimate Game Show	53
A Big Loss	54
Road Trip	58
Inside the Passage	59
Afternoon Tableau	61
Monkey and Snake	62
The Woods Grow Silent	63
Saving Life	66
The Beginning of the End	68
Funereal	69
The Jacceba Usurper	71
Misery	74
The Sermon on the Vault	77
The Moment of Capture	79
Oopsies	80
What a Life	82
The Lay of the Land	83
The Boarder Lady	84
Skull Session	87
That Was the Night	88
The Class Riots Resume	90
Setting the Woods on Fire	92
Force Majeure	93
A Big Grill Now	95
Eighteen Haiku of Arizona	96
Who Is It this Time	98
Fading Flower	99
Chain Reaction	100
Biting My Tongue	102

Generations	104
Talking Head	106
Inevitable	107
Los Mixtos	108
Keeping up with the Birds	111
Gored	113
A Post-Mortem Regression Digression	115
Nature, Friends, Is Boring	117
The Key	118
Respite	120
Deep in the Bunker	121
The Academician	123
Posted—No Entry	124
The Survivor State	125
Sunset on False River	127
After the Rig Collapse	128
A Category 4	129
The Woodman	131
Disharmonious Harmony	133
Ask if You Will	135
The Future Home of the Tabernacle of God	136
A Reincarnation	137
620 Conti Street	139
Acknowlegements	143

PREFACE

I believe that every piece of literature, regardless of form or style, should tell a story. Works that are so abstract as to be incomprehensible, or so esoteric as to be meaningless, even when containing beautiful strings of words or phrases, are of little value to me. After all, it is the oral tradition of story-tellers, or "griots," as we call them here in south Louisiana, that is the root of all written literature, ancient, old, or modern.

Thus, this book is a collection of story poems, some short, some long, each telling a tale, real or imaginary. They are written in wide-ranging styles of poesy; some are metered and have rhyme, some are in free verse, and some are hybrids approximating verse prose. These vignettes are drawn from life and experiences, native environs, imagination, and dreams, and I have tried to describe parallel universes existing within those sources.

So, sit back and take it easy while I tell you some stories.

John Lambremont Sr.

The Age-Old Struggle

Down where I come from,
you will see all kinds of things,
the real and the unreal,
the magnificently beautiful
and the fantastically ugly,
often close in place
and time, as if
by design.

One hot summer afternoon,
we drove down into the country-side
to take a ride along Alligator Bayou
(and, yes, that's its real name).
We pulled over and got out
to take in the swampy scenery,
and watched a man trying
to land a big catfish,
literally.

He was a small man,
neither young nor old,
and he had hooked the big one,
the kind of which great fish stories
are made. The fiery sun blasted a hole
through the thick canopy
of branches and leaves,
forming a golden halo
at the base of the steep bank,
a shining arena for the gladiators
of nature.

The man's light-tackle rod
was bent nearly in two,
and he tried to reel in the fish
without horsing it and causing
his ten-pound test line to snap and break.
He got the fish up to the bank

and tried to lift it out,
but it was much too heavy,
so, still clutching his rod with one hand,
he went to his knees to retrieve his catch
with the other.

When the fish hit the air,
it went into a flapping paroxysm,
thrashing and rolling
to try to throw the hook.
It was a huge channel cat,
thirty pounds or more,
and looked half as big as the man.
He dropped it onto the bank,
and tried to grab it with both hands,
and it promptly finned him deep,
blood spurting from a gashed thumb.
The fish rolled down the bank, slipping the hook,
and the man jumped on him
with a howl of pain and rage,
and the fight was on.

The man kept trying to drag the fish
up the ten-foot bank to level ground,
but the fish, fighting for its life,
kept breaking his hold and flopping back
toward the dark waters of safety.
The man, fighting for his dinner
and his pride, tackled the fish again
and again to haul it uphill,
a modern-day Sisyphus
with the slipperiest rock
imaginable. This went on
for several minutes until the fish
lay exhausted and still on the bank.

The man gathered his breath and his wits,
and sucked on his still-bleeding digit,
then picked the fish up for the last time
for the long haul to the gravel roadway above.
Halfway up the bank, the fish, playing possum,
lunged violently and broke free,
and once back on the ground,
with three large flops,
it hit the bayou water with a splash,
and was gone just like that.

The man crouched on the bank,
his thin shoulders heaving,
and I thought I heard him crying.

Embarrassed, we turned away,
and on the way back to the car,
I mused to myself,
"And so Nature abides."

The Paranormals

The water jug, set door-side, waits in dread anticipation
of what the owners might imbibe when they take in their ration;
some poison in a syringe, with a needle for direction,
delivered by a madman, would be their lethal injection.

The terrier runt, imprisoned in his new retirement home,
looks through the gate, ambivalent, as he eschews his bone;
he loves the tender preparations that the Missus fixes,
but to chew the Master's leg is what he truly wishes.

The broken-hearted chimenea stands out in the rain,
ignored by the owners, and frustrated by his name,
never having known flames or the comfort of hot coals,
and cloistered with the flower pots on the back patio.

The stately pine presides over the owners' house and yard,
but his pride's unfounded, as his insides are not hard;
some termites from Formosa have consumed his guts and brains,
and he will crush the owners in the next big hurricane.

The Day Our Home Exploded

It had been quite a Mardi Gras ride;
I'd gone off my pecan, fine dining
at Swifty's with the Stiffs,
devouring live crustaceans from
a car trunk turned aquarium,
then Hurricanes and Hand Grenades,
titty bars and lit parades,
ultimately a club crawl that left me
bawling on a dirty curb. I'd lost
my bag and laptop, and lost six months'
worth of work, and worse,
I didn't even have a shirt.

I trudged up the driveway; my mom
in the garage with her friends.
She told them, "Here comes my worthless son."
I just lost it; I went off on her,
cursing her angrily for her senility
and general bitchery.
I stopped when I saw how gone she was,
stars in her headlights, lipstick too red,
and equal parts poor Edith and her testy cousin Maude.

My sisters were shocked; one tore into me
savagely, another tried to be conciliatory.
I could only nod, and barely.
The little one, predictably, cried
like a baby.

Dad took me aside, took me outside,
and sighed. He spoke to me about being
an assistant professor of biology,
and showed me some slides of some
migratory microbes that had invaded
our seaside estuaries by attaching themselves

to mites that attach to fleas. Their radio-
optic colors were as pretty as could be,
but I had to tell my dad I don't know science
to any degree.

Dad glanced glumly up an old gum tree, and noted,
"This is the day that my home exploded."

One Southern Saturday

I had gotten so plastered at the tailgate party
that the ushers at the stadium wouldn't admit me;
I guess the wide splash of stinky puke
across my team shirt-tail and pants leg
was a dead give-away. I was stunned,
ninety thousand drunks filling
the world's largest bourbon vat,
all ready to watch the big game,
and I was too wiped out to get in.
I knew drinking all that tequila
was a mistake.

I stumbled back across what used to be
the campus golf course, trying in vain
to find the right tailgate,
but at night they all look the same,
and the specific gravity of alcohol
was pulling me down inexorably.
I reached the south highway,
and crossed over to the banquette,
kneeling helplessly as I puked again.
I knew that there was no getting up now,
and I crawled across to the southbound lanes
and tried to sit up against the rear tire
of a parked pick-up, but even this
was too much effort, as the spinning earth
pulled me flat,
and I lay on my back on the curb.

I could hear the crowd cheering,
and I thought about Yancey,
how he'd been run over and killed,
passed out drunk, on this same road
just after his eighteenth birthday,
and it took all my concentration
to keep from slipping off the curb
into the traffic lanes.

I heard my name being called,
and there was Rick,
wearing the same goofy Coca-Cola
beach pants and floppy hat
I'd chronicled in the student lit mag a year before.
He had been panhandling the tailgates,
asking for food, not money,
while he looked for something to steal during the game.
He held a gold pocket watch in one hand
and a half-eaten pork rib in the other.
He plopped down next to me,
and asked me what I was doing,
and when I told him,
his head rolled back in his hyena laugh,
his gnarled, yellow teeth illuminated
by the street lighting, and his shaggy hair
and long beard made him look like a
six-foot bespectacled gnome.
He showed me his shiny new acquisition,
and offered me the rib,
sticking the half-chewed bone
so close to my face that I
almost hurled again.

He sat on the curb, and we talked
as I lay there during the game,
reminiscing about great games and seasons past,
all the rounds we'd played on the old course,
about how all our rock heroes were dying
or dead, and we talked about Yancey,
and Scott, and Kevin, and our other friends
who had died too young.

Fans started streaming down the street,
homers happy and boisterous,
visitors sullen and silent.

A pretty coed in visiting colors
stopped to ask me if I was all right
before being jerked away angrily
by her fratty date, and I hoped her young evening
wasn't already ruined, then I felt
the sharp toe of a cowboy boot thump
against my ribs. I looked up into the face
of a hateful man dressed in visitors' garb,
and I realized that the truck we were under was his.
I scrambled away as he gunned the motor,
and I made it to my knees
as he spun around onto the asphalt,
nearly hitting Rick, who was making a hasty exit.

Rick screamed a curse after him,
and threw his rib as far as he could.
It hit the truck's team decal on the back window glass,
splattering barbecue sauce all over,
and fell neatly into the truck bed.

Corn

The threshing machines are all rolling around
eighty acres of stalks bayou-grown,
mowing down everything in their wide paths,
as if men were not at their controls;
and old Levon's jumping clear, with a mild grunt,
as if he's in a dream of his own,
chewing on my worn-out, half-eaten ear,
and bemoaning his want of some pone.

Feliz Año Nuevo

With tired smiles,
the two young wayfarers
on their way to Puebla
slink down the motel stairs
into the streets of Monterrey.

They have had a difficult day,
the crossing at Laredo
marred with missteps,
forgotten documentation,
and bribes to pay.
Finally underway,
they roared through the border
towns without a pause,
rubbing their hands together
in eager anticipation
of New Year's Eve
in the great city
of the northern mesas,
stopping only for gas
and more *cervezas*
on the straight highway
across the desert.

Freshened up and ready,
they troll up and down
the *avenida del centro*
all the way to the *zocalo*
and back, finding nothing,
all the *mujeres* already
on the arms of natives,
todo el mundo strolling,
singing, laughing, kissing.
The wayfarers are alone
in a crowd, ignored
and forlorn, soon giving up

and retreating to a café
for cheap *taquitos*
con salsa verde.

Long before midnight,
they are in bed,
unable to sleep
for the noise in the street
and the flashing reminder
of the red neon light
near their window.

Suburb in Rondo

1.

Sperm with no song,
sea plum trumpet,
now can you play?
Just one of those magic moments
you can never get back.

"Fire is the power in this patrol;
here return your bricks to home,
in travel and in stone."

I'm adapting to not adapting.
Woo me with passion, Mary Diamond,
I want it after the dirt.

2.

"Of course I can't tell
what this snap-out is made of,
but seeds sink into the loam
and lurk."

I see them in my mind
at the ten mark line;
I'm sawdusting
into the floor below.

My eyes want to be
a pair of hands that touch.
Let's try to war, it's called
a plot of goo.

3.

"Naturalism and diversity, is that correct?"
Pantomime flea stick tick dip?
The old cash register empty,
nothing that some money couldn't fix;
I'm a four-wheel chair on a five-wheel ramp.

"Want some smiley, some cerviche?"
I head shake, pensive in noodle soup.
Can I get some kind of bread,
just some kind of bread with this:
"That's no kid, that's a midget in spywear."

4.

"You're putting that in your navel?"
Oh, it's filling in nicely, I think.
Master of the breakfast table,
you can feel the passion in my stove;
the sausage is stuck in the sink.

We're staying down at the Cure-O apartments;
we need someone to re-mail these units.
"Ah, now I'm getting light-blinded;
I'm going to have to blink."

We'll check into
the gaudy pass-out truck,
assuming it's bawdy enough.

I might try the sticky round-up
and the parents' meeting,
to see if that will oppose,
as opposed to rope.

5.

"Now we go a-quarter hole digging,
nineteen holes, breast implant enhancement."
I see your view over the pushman leggings,
and it was short.

I will be pursued by your Rondo, even though
while I may move faster,
he will pursue faster also.

I will know the fullness of the river
when I feel the cool nest of the springs.

But the high tides of July
abound about the nineteenth;
encircle my gull cries,
as I might become extinct;
a last night's sojourn
as the moon turns full.

Deep Delta Freeze

The fishes stare up, pie-eyed,
sideways in the ice,
the brackish marshes frozen over,
satsumas in blight.

She fusses over grommets,
bungee cords, and tarps,
and mutters to the smudge-pots
that they won't save her crops

The tangerines are freezing,
and won't survive the night;
she glares skyward so angrily
she gives her God a fright.

The tall bananas withered,
their fruit hangs dead and brown,
so shriveled up and ruined,
one boot would bring them down,
but she won't do it now.

Small Favor

The first time he saw her stroll
slowly under the live oaks
and crepe myrtles on campus,
the lost look on her face convinced him
she was a refugee, newly-arrived,
fresh off the banana boat,
and he stared at her idly
out of curiosity.

She was of the better class,
her sweater, slacks, and flats
simple but fashionable,
her high cheeks very Oriental,
but not readily identified
by nationality. She was neither tiny
nor tall, her chin held high,
her eyes kept down.
Her round shoulders gave shape
to a cascade of long hair,
blue-black in its intensity
as it flowed gently down
her back. Sad and pretty,
her note-book pressed to her chest,
she passed him silently,
lost in thoughts
or memories.

He soon saw her again,
and then again; each time her allure,
foreign and exotic, became more evident.
It seemed every time he turned a corner,
she was there, always walking alone,
never talking or smiling,
and he realized she was no schoolgirl,
but a fully matured young woman,
older than he, who had lost it all
and was now starting over.

He began to look for her,
never going out of his way,
but becoming anxious
if she did not appear
for several days,
and when he spotted her,
he would stop to take in
her countenance once again.
Then one day, as he watched her walk away,
the soft sway of her hair and hips
caused lust to rage in his young head
and blood to rush though his loins.

He was confused and ashamed,
as he had already a girl,
and he didn't want to break up,
but there was something about
the refugee girl that he could not define
or ignore, and she kept showing up
in his dreams.

Late one afternoon, he saw her
trotting after a bus that didn't stop,
and as she gave up the chase,
he found himself approaching her,
a puppet without ties,
pulled by an invisible force.
He asked her if she missed her bus.
She said, "What?" and he knew
she knew little of his language.
He tried asking her name
and other simple questions;
she gave him a bemused half-smile,
but tried to answer him.
He could see now her imperfections,
one of her upper canines protruded,
and her eyes turned slightly inward,

but the whole effect was so winsome
and natural that it overwhelmed him,
and each time she said "What?"
his heart beat faster.

Ulinary Uprising

The first earth wave takes you by surprise,
and grabs you by the ankles,
the Ulinary undercurrent never stronger,
its waters thick and black as tar.
You know you must flee immediately,
or succumb.
You curse inwardly for having
dismissed your sitwas, and brace yourself
for an arduous escape.

The second earth wave takes you
by the thighs as you reach the crusted mounds,
wrapping its dark arms around you
to suck you in.
You claw your hands into the dried clay,
and strain for your life,
an inchworm pulling itself
from the muck of primordia.
You will not survive
the third earth wave.

The third wave breaks as
you free yourself and run for the cliffs
from the deadly tide.
From around the bend,
you can hear the cries of your subjects
on the public beaches.

You have climbed these bluffs
Since you were The Young Sajan, and know
all the footholds and handholds,
so you reach a safe height quickly,
then hear your name being called.
Below you on a sliver of ledge
are your wife and daughter.
You give them instructions,

but your wife is stupid
and the girl is timid,
and they stare up blankly,
not comprehending; but your sitwas arrive
with cords, pulleys, and rope chairs,
and you can turn your efforts to the horde
of sun seekers bolting up the dirt path
back to the city, some stained
by their own brushes
with death.

At the end of the trail
is a high rock outcropping,
and the commoners are fighting
over the ropes. A Fatweh woman
pushed perilously close to the edge
sees you, and whispers,
"Help me, Sajan,"
as the space for her feet disappears,
and she falls backward to her demise,
her robes flapping
in the updrafts.

You must take control,
so you run to the rock,
climbing it without a rope,
and shout, "This way!"
Others begin to follow
as you reach the city overlook station,
grunting in exertion and relief;
then you groan out loud as you peer down
at violent bedlam in your streets;
the Fatwehs and the Jaccebas are warring
again.

Rapture

From out of nowhere
                falls
a green dragonfly
                lying
at your feet in
the brown grass,
head and thorax still,
black lace wings
                    fluttering
in hot winds
                death

The Totality of Circumstance

The rebels trudge past the city gates,
stooping to collect the dirt bombs
they sowed so plentifully on their way in.
Between two palms, the bombs are placed with care
like a load of fresh-picked pears.
They are gathered and stacked in retreat
as a sign of a promise to truce despite
old grudges and new bruises.

The camera apprentice, Dufuisse, follows idly behind,
and finds a few more incendiaries.
Trying to be helpful, he puts them in his pockets
and deposits them on the burgeoning pile,
then turns away to cross over an old wood bridge
above the ravine to the landing
on the other side.

There, he looks back on the city at sunset,
a few fires from the fray still burning.
He reaches into his pocket for a roll of film,
and a discovers a dirt bomb instead.
He has no time to go back, as his master
is far ahead, and is glaring at him in impatience.

Dufuisse decides the best thing to do
is to lob the bomb across the crevasse
and bounce it up to the collected munitions,
but his throw is weak, and he stares in horror
as the bomb rolls back down the incline
and into the ravine, falling into a lean-to
built at the river's edge. It lands
in a cooking fire and explodes,
sending flames, ash, embers, and shrapnel
into the air above the wood bridge.
The palms all catch fire, and within moments
the entire pile of assembled explosives ignites.

A fireball erupts and rises, the blast concussive,
and Dufuisse covers his ears as the rebels, roaring,
turn and charge back across the bridges.
The loyalists pour out of the city gates,
and fighting, fierce and furious, resumes.

Dufuisse crouches down at the edge of the precipice,
then the ground beneath him gives way.
He slides down the dirt bank into the road,
where he is regaled by the foreign imperials
as a hero, but his name in his home country
will forever be a hissing and a by-word,
and he will live the rest of his life
in exile.

Screech

The neighbor macaw,
across the way,
gone off of his hinge
and completely deranged,
makes sounds just as strange
as any can be,
stuck in a cage
and out of his tree,
or is it just me?

Ungodly non-tunes
erupt from his craw,
like squirting balloons
rubbing raw on a wall,
a hapless old crone
being beat with a stick,
or a crying Afghani,
lead-poisoned,
death-sick.

I stand there dumb numbly,
lit nub in my maw,
and I wonder why
I went outside at all;
the raucous cacophony,
unnerving, reveals
a dark night refrain
of what daily I feel.

A Sequence

Surface

  just

    above

     him,

the diver pilot glides gearless,

    naked,

     waiting.

      Soon,

       soothing

        sea songs

         surround;   r   t

                  u   l

the green sea   t   e

        arrives, eyes passive.

         Hands slide to shell back,

          same hold as before,

           snout bubbles

            sustaining,

             they sail down

              soft currents to a

               sea bed, where

                to be decided

                 by the diver.

Foreign Beyond

The rescue boats are in retreat,
receding in blood sunset's glow,
and heading toward the Mother Fleet
so many leagues and months from home;
and he has been left here alone,
floating, helpless, in his dinghy,
and from ten score's cannons' roars
his reddened ears are roundly ringing.

He knows the tides of cruel night
will strand him on the foreign shore;
and so close to the rocks nearby,
his only hope now is to row
to one of the tall outpost trees,
to scale and hide away in wait
for fights to come tomorrow's day.

The trunk of the tree ends abruptly,
and he sees it's but a trap;
the tree, sprung, topples, and then throws him
in high flight toward darkened sands.
He lands in soft moss past the sea wall;
he is shaken but unhurt,
and wonders why he's not surrounded,
then his gaze is drawn off toward
the celebrating heathen sailors
cheering in their harbor's berths.

He must find shelter or be captured,
and runs to the nearest cottage;
there he finds an unlatched door,
and enters a top floor unlighted.
Peering down to rooms beneath him,
there on cots in woolen robes,
the Bony Crone and her four daughters,
and he shudders at these witches,
dangerous, and each well-known.

He creeps around to a side bedroom,
slips in quick, and shuts the door.
A moon-lit glass, and he sees water
he's not had since hours before.
He gasps at bitter-tasting liquid,
tries to spit, but it's too late.
The door opens, and a child enters,
featured by a candle's flame;
first she sees him, then she screams,
as he's the creature
known by name.

Out the window, in an alley,
the vile potion takes his sight.
He glimpses seraphim and maidens,
visions fading in his mind.
He slides his back along the boards,
and hides himself inside a trash pile.
There he feels the rats in scurry,
but he dares not now to stir; and
as he lies, the doubt of dying
does not once to him occur.

Fun With Shorty and Rondo

"You got anything in this condo, Rondo,
you know, that's strictly verboten?
As for you, Johnny,
you're my next torture victim,
and it ain't the lucky bamboo;
you ate all three chicken dinners."

My shoes are heavy at the thumbs.
I have no fingertips, I have no lips.
I only have ears for Shorty, the rest
is absorption.

Abasement

Sadly, you see
you are too late already,
the young lad, overwhelmed
by his failures on the pitch,
has been relegated
to a retention chamber;
there, he kicks his balls
disconsolately
in the corner
of a former
dug-out.

Even more horrific
is the cell-mate he's been given,
the Tweeter, equal parts human,
machine, and lemur,
whose gold eyes gleam
as he snaps off a bite
at the hand of your girlfriend
stuck foolishly through
the black painted chain-link.

You pull her aside,
but she stops to speak
to a chimpanzee peeking
through some broken ceiling tiles,
so you leave her behind.

You climb into your wobbly Buick,
engine turning over slowly,
and as you start rolling,
you disturb some hippies sitting
on their habitual curb,
but your path is impeded
by campus construction,
both roads and infrastructure,

and you don't know if
you have enough gas
to make it back home
with the stash
you have cached
in the quarter panel.

In the Interim

The young men pepper the precinct leader
with complaints of poor fortifications
and queries about reinforcements.

The old men scorn the younger,
who know not history,
who know not past failed moats
and scaled walls.

The precinct leader tries to maintain calm,
every few minutes trying again
to get through on the short-wave
to HQ.

The old women mutter curses
for the savagery
of the rebels, attempted genocide,
killing doctors, nurses,
medics,
and kids.

The young women sing soft
songs of old to the children,
held close in protective arms.

The children say nothing;
their eyes are wide.

Then the reports of guns and whistles;
the young men and women rise and
file by the militia arsenal,
picking up weapons to fire
proportionate to their size.

They slip out the side door
for another round
of fighting.

The elders take the babies, and wait.

Separate Classes

Two peas in a spoon,
two mystery pots,
her bright laughter rings
off chipped walls
and cracked windows.

She takes him in hand,
against the cold gray,
across to the grocer's,
and with his few dollars
buys staples and stew meat,
to make a small soup
of beef, groats, and whey.

After the repast,
he tries to romance her;
she demurs, quiet,
as they lie together.
Her face to his chest,
her almond eyes close,
and she takes a nap
under his watchful gaze.

Straining to be still,
his muscles are aching,
he strives not to wake her
until it is time;
he senses a process
that he hopes will progress,
and keeps himself quiet
until she arises.

Outside his apartment,
they find it is snowing;
it is her first snow,
and it seems like a sign.
They cross the wide campus

and pass the parade grounds,
while some foreign students
from yet warmer climates
are leaping and laughing,
and making first snowballs;
but she is older,
and has more reserve,
and soon they must part,
they are in separate classes.
They huddle together,
and trudge past the Union;
he feels her small breast
on his ribcage.

Food Fight

The apple smokes the bacon,
and blows smoke up the eel.
The eel becomes so toasty,
it makes a tasty sushi.
The sushi rolls on the apple
for the sweetness of the juice.
The juice then soaks the apple
for its fair share of the sauce,
and the sauce turns itself in
to some savory gravy
with which to bail the eel.

The apple, soured, smokes banana peel,
and soon turns yellow green.

I, Drunkie

My off-hand remark must have really cheesed
her off that time, because when I turned
from my window menu discussion with Rick,
she was gone, around the corner, and vanished.
I set off in chase, asking myself Why,
because I wasn't even
half drunk.

Rounding the corner, I ran down the hill,
splashing through puddles,
and trying to reach the bus stop
before I slipped and busted my butt,
but she was not in the bus line,
and the cab stand loomed across the street.
I wouldn't find her, at least not for now,
and as I reached for my flask, I wondered
if this was the last straw.

Rick sauntered up as I hit my whiskey,
and he murmured in his deep basso profundo,
"I've really got to get something to eat."
I nodded, waving him off weakly, and he strolled away,
shaking his head.

I hit the flask again, trying to console myself,
and humming an old soul song.
Suddenly, a tall black guy about my age
was next to me, singing the lyric,
and I answered in kind in the call-and-response style.
Soon, we were chatting, and he told me about a
cool record shop just up the block.
I offered him my flask on the way over there,
but he declined.

The record store was hip, with day-glow posters
and grooving music, and I told him I'd been wanting
for a long time to spend an afternoon
listening to that old R&B stuff
and getting very high.
He said he was down,
so we split for my apartment near the park.

"Nice pad," he said,
and sat on the edge of the couch
as I rewound a tape and gathered the fixings
for a big reefer. His eyes wandered around the room,
and he said, "Look, man, if you're sick, I know a guy."
I shook my head and told him I didn't use junk,
but he licked his lips and said, "I know a place where..."
and I realized, staring hard at the dingy edges of his brown face,
that he was just a junkie on the make.

Mercifully, the tape broke in rewinding,
and I seized this excuse for us to leave.
On the landing, I said, "If I was on junk, I couldn't do this,"
and then I tap-danced down the stairwell,
skittering out the front door
and down the street,
as I had no use
for a junkie.

Slipping Gears

The young girl at the corner
has her distress signals flashing;
she convulses sickly,
and appears to be grief-stricken;
both her hands are at her face,
and from where you're sitting,
the fading sun is making
all her rolling teardrops glisten.

Her side window is half-down,
so that when you pass her by,
you can hear the dreadful sounds
of gasping, full-blown cries;
something real has gone wrong,
broken car or broken heart,
and your heart goes out to her,
although you're worlds apart.

You mutter quietly to yourself,
like that would make it right:
"Keep your two hands on the wheel, girl,
try to hold on tight."

In the Aftermath
(for Salvador)

The bed of the Ulinary is desiccated,
devoid of its black tar flow now drying
in pools atop the surrounding bluffs
and outcrops of boulders and rocks,
a danger still to children and small animals.
The newer moon, so near in orbit
to cause the cataclysmic uprising,
reflects light so brightly that the night
is negated and the stars darkened.

Three Jacceba women, chosen muses
of the Citadel of Ancient Discovery,
are in search of exhibits swept away
by the dark toxic tide, their heads covered
to preserve their hair hues, but breasts bared
to absorb the beneficial moon
radiation, said to be lactary.

Two hold wooden torture instruments
from the Era of Insanity,
but the amalgahyde of the flood fluids
has rendered both pieces rubbery, while
the alloy sound weapon has brittled
and will disintegrate when touched.
The third waves to the Sajan's sitwas
waiting on a nearby ridge, a signal
for them to lower the ropes and nets
from their pulleys.

The Masher and the Maiden

```
The masher            young maiden
            and the

in tandem             Escher Tower,
            walk the

each step             no descent,
            down marking

his rude                        in turn,
          demands rebuffed

punctuated            tossing
            by her

one of his            red flowers
            proffered

down into             below;
            the streets

despite his                     threats
            naked, blatant

made from             of intents,
            the cruelest

she cannot            danger yet,
            sense the

and only              can save her.
            chance
```

John Lambremont, Sr.

Pachuco Y Juanito

Pachuco has brought into the cantina
his glorified version of a pellet gun,
a sawn-off muzzle-loading blunderbuss
able to shoot *todas tipos las cosas*.
He tells the barkeep he will use it
to keep a scavenging *gallina* out
of his novia's *casa de pollo*.
Juanito pales and stares at his
huevos, wondering
if el jefe del barrio knows.

Then the sound of a muffled discharge,
Juanito feels the stings of a dozen wasps,
and gasps, small metal pieces lodging
in his limbs. Raul darkens,
drops his few wrinkled bills onto the
vinyl tablecloth, murmurs, "*Vamanos*,"
and exits hurriedly, but Juanito,
picking a BB from his earlobe,
approaches Pachuco at the brass rail
and puts the projectile on the bar,
mumbling, "*Necessita tengar mas cuidado*,"
to which el jefe, his eyes narrowing,
replies, "*Y tu tambien*."

Raul *ha desaparecido*, the sidewalk empty save
Pachuco's *cadre de guerreros*. Juanito ambles down
the *paseo*, being followed, but once he passes
the *estacion de policia*, he is left alone
to pick shrapnel from his wounds.
His sternum is burning; probing
a cut, he extracts a small medallion
of *La Virgen*. He turns it over in
wonder, revealing *la marca 925*,
significa plata.

Juanito crosses over to the pawn shop,
as *La Virgen* will bring *dinero* for
tomorrow's dinner. Inside the door,
he considers his situation.
as it might be *mas mejor* to buy
with his last few *pesetas*
a matching silver chain.

Earth Invader

Quiet lunar ant-scape shattered,
giant's leather boot withdrawn,
chamber walls collapsing, battered,
sound the night air raid alarm.

Home defenders climb the ram-rod,
so to mount a vain assault,
workers start to move small dirt clods,
take unborns to deeper vaults.

Maidens cordon off Her Majesty,
try to keep her reassured,
just another routine tragedy,
nothing fire ants can't endure.

Kamikazes burn the enemy,
smoke billows, nostrils unfurl,
he rains down a gold tsunami,
drowns the Realm without a word.

Dummy

I'm just a dummy, but
I wasn't always.

I recall the day
I became this way,
my life of slime in the house
of Mary Diamond, her cavorting
with Shorty, and Rondo in wait,
the Drug Boys stealing what we
couldn't conceal, to buy more
habiturates to saturate primates
to capitulate to copulate.

I couldn't take any more, the final straw
was a bedlam free-for-all with Mary
and Shorty and Band Anna in cocoon,
live larvae wiggling in phyllo sheets
that my hands tore away, with Rondo trying
to look the other way.

Mary cried as we said good-bye,
time enough for last snorts at
the Quark Bar, Shorty in there gambling
for Rondo with Ratman, and Ratman losing
as Rondo looked on. Ratman accused me
of slipping Shorty a tip, he whipped
me with his pistol, snapping,
"What you doin' back there, dummy!"
and running out the front door.

Shorty and Rondo and the parking lot
armed guard in pursuit, Rondo
in his Springboks, Shorty in his flip-flops,
pseudo-cop's boots loose from his spool of
dirty sox, me barefoot and tripping
on tree roots. Ratman tried to scale the Lynx

fence, tried to be past tense, pulled
out his gun and shot straight at me;
I've been a dummy ever since.

His bullet hare-lipped me and cleft
my palate, coming to rest in the back of
my neck; I lost connect before
the doctor left, Shorty asking him
what was next; the doctor said
I'd have no voice left due to damage
to my left side cerebral cortex.

Now I spend my days digging quarter-
hole on video, no breast implant
enhancement. Shorty keeps my
winnings; he says it takes a lot of money
to keep a Rondo and a dummy, and
he should know.

At night, I write words I've heard
from the slug in my chamber, itself
their lone arranger:
"Oriental shortstop
gastronomic polyglot,
samurai drive trough,
jellyfish matzo balls,
Tokyo cyclos
form a centipede that grows,
zebra skin sky glows,
pig foot refusal,
menu perusal,
not enough tofu,
get the Mac-Rib-A-Knack
greased in Febreze."
Mary says they're
fairy pomes, and puts them on

her Face; Shorty says they're
crap, but will attract stranger
strangers.

Mary lets me play push-cart
on the shag carpet, and once
straddled me quietly at night in
her gown. Shorty says if Rondo knew
what was going down, he'd slay
both our stray asses; but
fortunately,

I'm just a dummy.

The Gift

He bought his wife a Valentine,
a miniature azalea bush,
its tiny flowers reminiscent
of their first few bashful kisses,
sash and bow somehow symbolic
of their marriage vows.

They left it on the counter-top,
and so admired it every day,
but after a week-end away,
they found it brown and dying.

He hastened it into the ground,
and felt blessed by an early spring,
but one of dryness nearing drought,
so he did water copiously,
and waited for the roots to take,
for in his superstitious way,
he felt the shrub's demise might mean
the loss of things rings signify.

He waters the plant night and day,
as yet, to-date, there's been no rain,
but the azalea won't revive,
and, dull and brown, may not survive;
does he give it enough loving?
Or too much? He cannot say.

Batter Whipped

It's a long drive back
after a loss when
you're o-fer with
two Ks looking.

You drive by the old Sunbeam bakery,
bricks peeling paint,
a former name-brand product
and icon of local prosperity,
now a faded reminder of
a frazzled city's shaky economy.

Their schtick had been
their batter-whipped bread,
whipped to remove air bubbles
for a smooth interior loaf, slices
that tore right down the middle,
just like on T.V.

And the aroma of fresh bread
never changes, and recalls
your fourth-grade field trip,
details now cloudy,
but the aroma, ah,
the wonderful smell
of flour and yeast and
dough all rising together in
batter-whipped splendor,
a small loaf given
to each of you
as a parting gift.

That night, after your D-League Legion game
(your team whipped by Bet-R Stores,
you with no hits, two strikeouts looking,
and a missed bunt),

mother made tuna sandwiches
and let you and your sisters tear
in perfect halves, just like on T.V.,
a few slices saved for toast tomorrow.

You're in bed in your Reds pajamas,
but burning temptation
overcomes trepidation.
You sneak into the dark kitchen
and hold the last slice over the garbage pail.
You pull it into one more beautiful split,
then are frozen as the invisible mother
in the T.V. room calls out,
"Stop tearing up bread
or you're going to be whipped!"

You cringe, apprehended, in
sudden fatal comprehension:
you're a bad batter,
a worse boy, and the worst son ever,
and you are going straight
to hell.

Ultimate Game Show

The answers,
it was explained,
  would be

      dropped
        onto
     a whirling
    mirror-ball of
     questions
    by means
       of
a series of
telepathic
  threads
         unseen.
When it was
      pointed out
that it would be near-
         impossible
to determine a winner,
and that the game might
      go on
         forever,
the toothsome emcee
gave the perceptive
    contestant
        a c   y grin.
           h   s
             e e

A Big Loss

I have to leave the apartment,
and I tell my wife I have to go
to the Law Center to
write a brief, so she says,
"Then don't be long."

She is trying to clean up
water color puddles on the floor,
and pick up the brushes and books
and clean off the kids,
and she says Uncle Xuan
is coming for dinner and asked for pho,
and the beef bones for the broth
are boiling in the kettle,
and Nguyet and Phiet are coming
to spend the weekend, but Tiffany's off
with the Girl Scouts somewhere..

So I jump into my Mustang
and head off toward campus,
but I end up way up Stanford
at a bar and grill in the Dales,
as I've got to make a quick pick-up,
so I park and jump out,
and the bar is crowded,
everybody's excited about the street party festival,
and I don't have time, so
I go back to the curb,
and I can't find my Mustang,
and I haven't been drinking.

On the crowded sidewalk,
I run into Rick, and I tell him
I can't find my Mustang,
and I haven't been drinking.
and he doesn't care,

he won a radio contest,
and he's going to meet Willie Nelson today,
and here comes Willie
and his entourage in tow,

and the people are hip-to-hip,
so they have to pass
the equipment overhead,
and someone passes me
a battered guitar case,
so I start walking, and they're worried,
I'm not their roadie after all,
but I just carry the box
down to the corner chapel
where the church musicians
are all tuning their bells and finger cymbals
and triangles and such,
and I hand it up to Willie himself
in the belfry. I look out to Stanford,
and there's a donkey race going on,
but the donkeys are tied together
and keep falling down,
and their riders fall off.

So I cut across the field,
and the Who is in concert,
but the freaks turn their backs
and the field is empty,
then I see Moon drumming,
and I know it's a copy tribute band,
what Moonie dead all these years,
plus four more Who in old mod gear
among the cheerleaders,
so I cut back to the street,
looking at every parked car,
but it's like my Mustang is gone,

and the flat Dales sidewalk is full,
I keep bumping into people,
and I worry my buddy bag might fall out,
so I adjust my gym shorts,
and go back through the bar,
there's a back parking lot,
and the carpenter's drunk
after fixing the patio deck,
and I try to tip-toe by,
but he sees me and hollers
in Ecclesiastics and Psalms,
so I just walk away,
and there's a long bed tow truck
with custom new Mustangs on it,
but mine is old and green
and has a dented front fender
and bumper stickers all over
the back end.

So I go around the corner,
but I can't get back to Stanford,
and I walk down near the campus,
descending into the record store,
and the longhair musicians
are tuning up their cellos and
violas and tympani and such,
their tuxes and gloves all shiny;
I am in the way,
and I don't have time,
so I enter the Highland gates
to try to get to the Law Center,
but the gate leads into
a labyrinth of hallways,
and I'm lost.
I walk through double doors
into an exhibit about tugboats on the river,

and I step out onto a boat's bow
and marvel at the graphics,
but the chlorinated water burns my airways,
and the mechanized rocking is making me sick.

Road Trip

Expressions of shoulders
confirm road-map choices,
depressions of verdancy
gap peaks of brown;

chattering magpies,
all filled up with French fries,
are deep asleep, silent,
as we enter town;

and then, past a bend,
we find vendor men waiting,
their swaying gondolas
will bring us straight down

to a cluster of cabins,
old brownstones, and carriages;
what was a mining store,
now House of Clowns.

Inside the Passage

A space, whether large
or small, remains a space,
and largely defines a place.

The inner berth is a small
and windowless place,
but there is enough space
for two beds, a closet,
and a full bath. Its pitch
is much less than that
of the balcony suites
out by the bow,
as is its price.

The immense banquet hall,
boasting its Stilton, lox,
au jus, and tasty pastries,
is accessed by an entry
so slender as to be clogged
by two old codgers with walkers.

The salmon of Ketchikan
flee the vast sea to climb up
narrow river ladders,
and join their siblings
gathered in one small space,
the place where they are born,
return to spawn, and pass on.

The small capital of Juneau
has no roads in or out,
no airport, and no tall spires,
but the bars are full,
and the natives are lively.

The glaciers are huge,
cold, and ice blue,
and impress on you
the idiocy of trying
to hike them or fly atop
in a helicopter.

The mountains that surround,
green from sky to ground,
provide a scenic backdrop
for nature's chicanery,
rolling otters, an awkward walrus,
the crash of a splashing stray whale,
but, in time, your eyes start to strain,
the vistas, so clean and pristine,
never end, like a strange dream,
and you see through the panorama
of evergreen that you are trapped,
a small animal on an ornate treadmill,
afloat in an elaborate palace
of purgatory.

Upon embarkation
at the end of your vacation,
the long road to Anchorage
provides more of the same,
and you wonder whether or not
everything has changed;
then, rounding a sharp bend,
you glimpse the golden scallop
of a new Shell service station;
your breathing comes more easily,
you begin to feel normal again.

Afternoon Tableau

Lester blows the melody softly
deep down in the box, as Oscar
and his trio comp and follow.
A warm solo saunters
through the heat of the room
and slides past the open drapes
out to the street-car riders below.
The all-star quartet is now nearly done,
but it's the two tiny table dancers
that can't get started.

Faded flower lady and tinker-toy boy
lean on each other listlessly,
already in a sweat from the exertion
of erectness, their stick limbs
near breaking with the want to stretch.
They cannot find the time, but blindly seek
the beat entwined, their feet colliding
in a clumsy shuffle on the table-
cloth checker-board dance floor of vinyl;
together they sway in languorous dolor,
an impromptu, unrehearsed dance recital.

The music stops, and so do they;
they stand, hand-in-hand, and panting.
The man in the box booms
be sure to stay tuned, as
the son of Silver will play soon
a song for his father.

Still on their feet, they
wait for the suite, and
pay close attention
as they feign disaffection.

Monkey and Snake

I am a Monkey,
my wife is a Snake.
That's just the way
the old fortune cookie breaks.

I am highly intelligent,
able to influence people,
an enthusiastic achiever;
but I avoid Tigers, as
I am easily confused
and discouraged.

My wife is wise and intense.
She is physically beautiful,
vain and high-tempered;
the Cock is her best companion.

My wife's people say
a Monkey and a Snake
are a bad match,
as monkeys try to jump
from tree to tree,
and snakes like to bite.

I think they're right.
I should know:
we've been matched now
for thirty-six years,
and sometimes I cry
96 Tears.

The Woods Grow Silent

She had stood alone for so long,
watching her deciduous forest grow,
that the first filing seemed a relief,
as children are more lively
than are rabbits and moles.

Homes too hot to stay in,
yards too hot to play in,
kids took refuge in the parasol
of her broad-leafs' shadows,
an ancient noble live oak
the center of the compass
of her known world.

Its vine became a swing,
across a ravine and back,
its wide roots platforms
for making the leap.
Boards nailed into its huge girth
made rungs to climb up
to broad branch benches.
The boys made bike paths
in and around the valley,
and a campsite developed
at the height of the upper loop.

Her lagoon taught the children
about water-striders and dragonflies,
terrapins and moccasins,
and her meadow was full of dandelions
and dewberries ripe for picking.
The boys chopped and stripped thistle
for the crunchy inner ring,
and the girls gathered acorns for
biscuits and sought chanterelles
under the shaded ivy of slopes.

But, as the great poet once said,
"Nothing gold can stay,"
and slowly things changed.

Boys were smoking grapevines,
then stolen cigarettes, a careless match
burning up half the meadow
one hot and dry August day.
Stick guns became air rifles,
and play forts became shanties built
from stolen construction materials.
Bad boys took foolish girls
under the boughs, out of sight,
for awkward attempts at intercourse,
and later, three deranged brothers
took the autistic boy up the old oak
and used his arms for an ashtray
and his head for a urinal.

By then, the houses had window units,
and the kids were forbidden to enter her,
and stayed away. Once again she stood alone,
until the second filing came.

Her meadow, ravine, and lagoon
were all bulldozed and leveled,
and the sacred oak of centuries
was toppled and set ablaze.
But a part of her remained,
a secret to a lucky few,
beyond a hedge of cane-brake,
a large cypress swamp-lake
of more than forty acres,
a place of egrets and alligators
and quiet.

That part of her is preserved
as a city-owned wildlife center,
with overlooks and walkways,
and a hall with bright exhibits;
her park bears the bluebonnets' name.

Saving Life

The widow's heart and soul had been saved
in a small black box, firm but flexible,
no bigger than a picture book,
complete with a viewing screen.

I tried to seat her
to get her basic information,
but the box seemed to have
a life of its own, twisting and
flopping over. Finally, I placed her
in the baby chair, a refurbished piece
of nostalgia from the infancy
of our first-born.

Her wizened face on the small screen
appeared to be mumbling,
but I could not hear her.
I turned the volume knob
all the way to the right,
to no avail.

Suddenly, the screen went blank,
and a red indicator light came on.
The box began emitting loud, urgent beeps,
and the tell-tale initials CVI flashed
on and off on the screen.
I knew instantly, despite no experience,
that she was having a heart attack.

I snatched her up and put her under my arm,
shouting to my wife to call an ambulance
to meet us en route to the General Hospital.

Out the back door and down the side stairs
I scampered, jumping into my car, and screeching
my tires as I pulled out of my parking space.

Coming around the corner of the building,
I saw the ambulance driver at the top of the stairs.
I stopped and jumped out, calling him down,
and placed the box, now still and rigid,
on the hood of my car.
He ambled down slowly,
and assayed the situation
with a detached hum.
"Sometimes, you have to wonder
why we even bother," he stated.
Noting my exasperation, he went to his vehicle,
retrieved his laptop, and plugged it into the box.
He then typed on his keyboard for awhile.

The screen came back on, and he said,
"She'll be all right, at least for now."
I looked at the screen, and the old woman
was sleeping peacefully, and smiling.

The Beginning of the End
(for Soren)

The first cicada of the season
goes off like a fire alarm;
near my window, strident trills
mark his flight from summer prison,
harping of the Fall to come;
his micro-pauses belie hope
of return to tranquil July.

Ominous, imminent, shrill, and prescient,
buzzing like a toy time bomb,
his warped incessant incantations
wreck my midnight reverie and
rattle all my thoughts;
I am filled with Fear and Trembling,
and sense The Sickness unto Death.

I still hear it in bed later,
listening to my rasping breaths,
a tinnitus of Soul.

Funereal

Exiting the municipal building,
I quickly light a cigarette,
nicotine cravings overwhelming,
but as I cross over into the park,
strolling and puffing under
the high rose arbors in bloom,
I realize a funeral is underway,
so I extinguish my butt;

for the old albino negro has passed,
and his five sons, in their high-
buttoned suits, sit on the parlor chairs;
wiry-haired and mustached, they are multiples
of each other, albeit of different ages.
They sit solemnly and stare at the grave,
even though the funeral is over and
most of the mourners have left.
They will sit for most of the after-noon,
while their darker female kin
sit in camp chairs off to the sides,
tapping their feet, whispering,
and tending to the little ones.

I marvel at their stoic faces and
the firmness of their last respects,
unwavering in the summer heat.
My mind goes back to funerals
I've attended; how quickly dispersed are
the well-to-do to their air-conditioned
Caddys and Porsches and hearses! and then for this
I am saddened, and my eyes form tears
which I brush impatiently away.

I stay and watch awhile, though
there's nothing, really, to watch, just a
fervent and reverent feeling to be absorbed,
if possible. I stand under the tall cypress,
and as I look down, I realize that the tree root
beneath my feet is the same one I saw
when I first came here.

The Jacceba Usurper

In the darkness between
the setting of the large moon
and the rising of the small one,
he slips into the women's chamber,
idly, without thinking.
His brother's wife sleeps separate
from the women lined on pallets.
She has assumed the waiting position
in the ritual rope bed,
half kneeling, half crouching,
arms extended, hands on the supports.

He sees she is sleeping lightly,
her lashes flutter slightly,
and he wonders why his brother
has not taken her;
two days have passed
since their vows were exchanged,
and she is a handsome woman,
beamy, roomy, and able.
He had wanted her for himself,
but she had favored his brother,
said the village chief,
and he could not understand this,
as he and his brother were identicals.
He sensed the presence of politics,
since his brother was a sitwa in training,
soon to be pressed into service
to the Sajan.

He stands above her, longing,
then pulls a small stool over
to the head of the bed.
Up on it, he sees an opening
between her arms and chest
big enough for his slim frame.

He steps gently over the supports,
and slides slowly beneath her,
then realizes immediately
he is trapped.

She feels him pressed against her, and stirs.
A pleasant sound escapes her
as she embraces him,
and he buries his face
between her heavy breasts,
in case the dark
does not allay detection.
Every part of him is petrified,
including his maleness.
She pulls aside her bed robe
and loosens his loincloth,
lowering herself onto him.
She moves slowly on top of him,
kissing his long neck
to muffle her moans.

He hears a sound above them,
and looks up in the soft light
of the rising second moon
to glimpse the face of the elder vesper,
who watches without expression.
Again he hides in the bosom
of his brother's wife, until
he hears the vesper clear her throat
quietly and leave the chamber.

His brother's wife has not noticed,
so deep is her passion,
and he is soon astonished
by the quickness and force
of his climax. She removes herself,

and lays back on the bed
in the rapture of the moonlight,
her tureen at full brim.

In the early morning,
he enters the meal chamber,
and sees his brother's wife
smiling and making love eyes
at his brother, who ignores her
as he eats with his fellows.
At the head table, seated
between the chief and the elder vesper
is the Sajan himself.
The Sajan has a smile for the villagers,
but peers at him intently,
no laughter in his eyes.

Misery

Your wife is tired
of running through airports,
and nearly missing (or missing) flights,
so you go two hours early,
but as boarding time approaches,
there is an announcement:
your plane has developed
mechanical problems,
and will be two hours late.
You now will miss
your connecting flight.

They give you a voucher
for free airport food
(alcohol excluded),
but you wait in line
to find out whether you
can catch another flight
or otherwise make connections.
The process is slow, aggravated
by unending questions posed
by insecure woman travelers
who (save one) cannot understand
the simplest of options
or make up their minds,
and you do a slow burn.

It is finally your turn,
and the counter woman says
she thought you were transferred
to the 6:45, but it is 6:45 already,
no one called your name or destination,
and your last chance to be re-routed
is gone.

Your choices, then, plain and simple,
are to stay the night where you are,
or make the first leg of your trip tonight,
finishing tomorrow. You choose the latter
quickly and head out for some food,
as your plane has finally arrived.

The food lady is surly and slow.
and doesn't want to validate the voucher
and your food choices are limited,
but you want hot food that isn't junk,
this is dinner, after all.
By the time you get back to your gate,
the plane is already boarded,
and your wife is already
pissed off.

Your carry the food on,
and try to eat as the plane takes off,
but the food, while warm, is awful.
You shovel it down; this is dinner
(after all), but your wife picks at it,
then slams it in disgust
into the plastic bag you proffer.

The red-headed man across the aisle
is tall and handsome, and you glance at him
a few times, as does your wife.
He reads a magazine, and has a vodka tonic,
as he does not have a drinking problem.
You have a ginger ale.

Your wife puts her purse in her lap,
and curls her arms over it,
closing her eyes tightly shut,
but she is not asleep.

You long to retreat into slumber,
but there is turbulence outside the plane, too,
and the window glass is freezing your shoulder.
There is no escape, and you question why
you try to get away at all,
or even live.

The Sermon on the Vault

The sermon was on a youth of the parish,
who, through faith and technology,
had set a parish record in the vault
by using a new and improved pole;
but my mind strayed back to my young attempts
with hand-cut cane poles on homemade stands,
and old mattresses as a landing pad,
so I missed the point.

Later, the lone usher asked me,
although I was a stranger,
to help carry the offerings to the altar.
I was given a crystal cruet of red wine,
and walked with the others to the pastor.
Blessing us, he left through a side door,
and white curtains parted to reveal
a high-definition large-screen Vizio
equipped with a pod camera.

The pastor's face appeared on the screen,
and he made his benedictions.
As I genuflected nervously, the vessel's
stopper fell out, and most of the sacrament
spilled on the carpet, making a stain.
I saw his scowl on the screen, and apologized,
wiping up the blood of Christ
with my handkerchief, but he said nothing,
summoning the flock to the Eucharist,
and, although the line was short,
there was none left for the last, me.

After the service, I saw in the parking lot
the young vaulter's rig, scaffold-like
and rising to a platform.
In a brace next to it stood
his renowned synthetic pole,

John Lambremont Sr.

which I took gingerly in hand
and hefted toward the heavens.
I ran toward the vault, hitting the
box perfectly, feeling the bend
of the pole, and thrusting my legs
toward the platform as high as I could,
but once again I failed the leap of faith,
falling backwards, but landing on my feet.

Then the long, black hearse
with the dark-tinted windows
started rolling, directly at me,
and I thought, "Now I'm in real trouble."

The Moment of Capture

Many Asiatic peoples
take memorial snapshots
of their elders,
commemoratives to gap
the ages. The best clothes
and best chairs are deployed
for the permanent portrayal.
These revered images will rest
on hearths forever, or sometimes as
the centerpiece of a shrine
in Buddhist homes, duplicated
for the family temple of choice.

My wife's mother sits in
a white chair, her blue gown
a special hue reserved for
relatives of the last emperor.
She knew this was the moment of capture.
Her countenance mixes calm
and annoyance, as she was a remnant
of an gone era, her betel-
stained black pearls hidden
behind pursed lips. Her face
shows resignation, or,
perhaps, the burn of the tumor,
yet undetected,
that would take her away.

Oopsies

Dean and Nancie,
after a ten-year hiatus,
were having an inadvertent third try
at parenthood, and the genetic dice
came up Girl once again.

They let me take the zygote,
ex utero in a petri dish,
down the block to Emily
to get her first look
at her little sister,
and on the way back,
I dropped it.

It slid out the dish
and hit the sidewalk,
breaking the yolk.
I went to my knees in panic,
but grateful that the sun
was not so hot as to cause
burn damage. My wife appeared,
and tried to help me.
We systematically picked up the pieces,
and put the yolk back together,
making sure not to miss
a single strand of chromosome.
We added a tube of amniotic fluid
and some extra agar, stirring gently.
Then I noticed the single yolk
now looked like two.

When we were done,
the thing looked all right,
but it was impossible to tell,
and would take weeks to know
if the foeti were still viable,
or whether there would be deformities.

My wife saw my grief,
and tried to console me.

"It will be all right," she said.
"It came out all right with Sarah."
I didn't know how
I could face Dean and Nancie,
but I knew they had to be told,
and I didn't know what to say.

I always felt Dean disliked me.
Now he would have good reason
to hate me.

What a Life

A domicile that's still preferred
in every city and major burg;
a nice home on a quiet street,
lawns all kept well and clipped neat;
regardless of the random names,
all the houses look the same.

In every front yard, near and far,
the high pines and the callous tallows
keep the young oaks short and fallow;
they do not allow passage of
the sun's bright and sustaining rays;
in a singular tilt toward an early grave,
the oaks have nowhere left to turn,
and suffer the dirty burn.

Now I watch, and I am torn
as jays chase sparrows from their trees,
my lack of spirituality
envelopes my dualities;
Where am I now? Are my thoughts heard?
Everything is in its place,
but it's unreal and I'm absurd.

The Lay of the Land

Smiles break out across my face,
as stems break off in my hand.
Rotted fruits are hiding below,
as I'm learning the lay of the land.

Rueful, I remember well
the hours of pickaxe sweat,
weeding until numb,
and eventual neglect.

The lone radish grown was one too many,
smelling foreign, nearly poison
because of the lay of the land.

My summer garden
akin to my adulthood,
unplanned and squandered,
still borne in utero.

I fondle clots of soil,
smoking stains on my fingers
already darker than the dirt.

Beyond the rose arbor
the reaper awaits,
leans on his tool,
picks his stone teeth,
and drools, as
he knows well
the lay of the land.

The Boarder Lady

Soon after I entered the big house,
I was brought to her dark,
antiqued sitting room.
She gestured to the dying fire,
and said, "Throw a board at it."

After some initial confusion,
I went over to the fireplace
and put a log on the hearth,
as she explained the origin
of that unusual phrase.

There had been, she related,
a young man of the county,
her neighbor since childhood,
who was no one's fool.
He shunned school and
scoffed at convention, self-
educated and independent,
and he dabbled at farming
while distilling white lightning
in a rig that would make
a chemistry professor envious.
His pappy had taught him
the recipe, and his tinkering
with vessels, tubing, and vats
had perfected it. Highly prized
for its potency and purity,
its sale and consumption
had provided him a good life
over the years.

Eventually and inevitably,
his reputation as a master maker
caught up with him, and brought him
unwanted attention. She,

her father, the sheriff, and the mayor
all warned him that the revenuers
and the ATF boys were tough
and did not play, and,
unlike the local Police Jury,
would not look the other way.

On the eve of the raid,
forewarned and pre-ordained,
she begged him to dissemble
the works and pour out its contents,
but he'd refused, and when
she asked him what he would do,
he said he was going to throw
a board at it.

The G-men were in the barn,
tapping planks, looking for the
hidden chamber holding the rig.
He waited until the last moment
for the timed fuse
to light the dynamite,
then lit out in a dead sprint
as the explosion blew out
an interior wall, dislodging
the boards and disabling most
of the plain-clothed searchers,
but a handful of them escaped
injury, and their precise shots
cut him into ribbons and threw him
up against the barbed-wire fence
he'd put up to keep out
poachers.

She paused for a minute, tears forming,
and I knew she had loved him, even though

he was not of her station
and could never have married her.
"I bought the estate,
and converted the house into a
boarding school for boys,
but I never did any good with it,
so I threw a board at it.
This banner is all that's left.
Then I sold the land to the county
for the community college.
That's where you come in."

She rose stiffly,
shuffling behind her walker,
and left me there alone.

I got up and examined
the hanging banner marked
"Manning School For Boys.'
A sniff of the wrinkled yellow cloth
revealed the unmistakable aroma
of kerosene, and I wondered if
she'd even filed an insurance claim,
as she didn't need the money.
I pulled back a corner of the banner,
and found taped to the back
an old faded photograph
of them as teenagers.
They were holding hands.

Skull Session

The dog tags told me what it was
before it touched my hand,
taken from a folded baggie,
a chunk of a jet pilot's skull plate,
a curved human coconut shell,
once-dark hair a green patina
that crumbled at the touch.

He'd brought them back from a trip home,
his nephew found them in wreckage
hidden deep in a Quang Tri ravine,
undiscovered for years after the war,
hidden for a two decades,
until the elder returned.

He asked me what he could do with them,
perhaps a grateful America would bring across
his brother and nephew and niece,
or maybe there was a cash reward.
But he knew if the feds in Ha Noi
or their goons in Sai Gon caught wind
of what his people had kept secret,
they'd face prison or death or worse.

Turning the skull-piece over in my hand,
my thoughts went out to the M.I.A.'s family,
their not knowing his fate
during the intervening years;
but my duty was to my client,
so I kept his decision buried deep
in this aging skull of mine.

That Was the Night

It was well after midnight;
I was still up, on-line,
on a local message board.
I can't recall whether the talk
was next year's quarterback
or whether Peart was better than Moon.

My mother was in the next room, dying.
I could hear her labored breathing
through the open door. Like her brother,
she had shunned the chemo and radiation,
knowing that the few extra months
would be a rough road down
to the same dead end.
I was glad she was deep in an opiate sleep,
and that she hadn't suffered terribly.

My sister and her husband slept in the front room.
We all wanted to stay that night;
we knew it was going to be, most probably,
her last.

I noticed the house had grown quiet.
My mother was no longer breathing.
I felt guilty, but ambivalent.
I found no irony in the fact that she'd died
as she'd lived after the divorce, alone,
and I did not rationalize when I surmised
that she would have preferred to pass
without us at her bedside.

I got up to attend her,
but I had to go first to the bathroom.
It didn't matter anymore, anyway.
While I was washing up after,
I noticed from under the door

that the hall light was on. As always,
my sister was there first,
and as I opened the door, she said,
"She's gone."

Mom didn't look dead, only tired.
I closed her eyes, and wiped some
spit-up from her lips.
My sister went to call the hospice
and rouse her husband.
I took a rose from the vase,
and laid it lengthwise on Mom's gown,
which made my sister cry a little.

The hospice lady arrived at four,
and we prayed, that is to say,
they prayed and I prayed along.
Then the funeral home guys came
and put a sheet over her,
and it struck me that I'd never
see her again, as she wanted
to be cremated.

I went outside and watched them
load her into the wagon and drive off.
As they made the corner,
the cold November fog and street lights
and trees began to blur. I bit my lip
as a thought coursed through me:
"This is the night they took my mother away."

The Class Riots Resume

Mr. Lenny offers as refuge
his family's apartment on Dumaine
or their camp in Cocodrie,
but I remind him through my transcriber
that if the mob recognizes him
as a rich executive in hiding,
his family may need the refuge
for themselves.

As I load my transport,
the Ratman anthem rap starts seeping
out of every personal and transport
audio player within earshot,
and the poor whites and browns
and blacks filter out of their tenements,
brandishing antiquated Glocks and
Kalashnikovs, and gather quickly
in the street with a sense
of purpose.

I am noticed immediately,
and a dozen of the rabble approach,
breaking into a run as I jump into my transport
and activate the engine.
I have barely enough time
to flip the shields on and roar away
as old-fashioned steel-jacketed projectiles
splat on the shields.

Rounding the corner, I see Shorty and Band Anna
hiding behind a bush. I stop and let them in,
the mob behind me chasing on foot.
Shorty sweats and curses as he tells me Rondo has been captured
and re-programmed by Ratman,
and Anna is in tears, so scared
she is biting a hole in her bottom lip.

Before I can transcribe to Shorty
about what should we do,
we see a roadblock of wrecked transports ahead.

Rondo stands atop the pile, and his face
sports a hideous grin I'd never seen
in all our time with him.

"Ram him," commands Shorty,
and when I hesitate, he hollers,
"Now, Dummy!"
I set the transport to maximum acceleration,
and pray the shields hold up
as we careen toward the iron pile.

With a sickening screech of shields on metal,
we plow through the mountain of wreckage,
then slow to a crawl as the engines sputter.
The shields have failed,
and the mob is on us in an instant,
banging on the transport,
its armor our only protection.
Before us stands Rondo, and he laughs.
Band Anna lets out low death moans.
Shorty shoves me aside with a "Move, Dummy!"
and tries desperately for re-ignition.
I want to scream, but, of course,
I can't.

Setting the Woods on Fire (an Acrostic)

Strike a match and drop it down,
Easy catch to patch of thatch;
Then you call your friends around,
They see fire spreading fast,
Igniting the field of brown;
Now your faces are aghast, you're
Going to burn the whole woods down.

Take off shirts to beat the flames,
Hope dies as the flames rise higher,
Every bad kid plays with fire.

While you run for grown-up help,
Only thought is of your shame,
Only blame is on yourself,
Doing things that show no brains,
Stupid self-inflicted pain.

Once the neighbor men arrive,
Not long 'til they kill the fire.

Fourteen acres you've burned up;
In anger, with biting words,
Red men chide you, you dumb cluck;
Ever will you hear these words.

Force Majeure

Sunless and near Bible-black,
the heavens hurl rain at the coast;
waves batter the shoreline,
slamming against the pilings
supporting the beach house.

Evacuation was not mandated,
the hurricane only Category Two,
and their supplies were plentiful,
a new generator purchased,
so they'd planned to stay and make camp,
to rough it, so to speak,
to ride the storm out,
novice pioneers in the final frontier
of retirement.

His wife was uncertain,
and he too has doubts
as the tidal surge begins
and breakers crash higher,
overlapping the back deck.
Already the beach has disappeared
beneath the swarming gray seas.

Then a huge swell hits the deck
and knocks down the screen door,
flooding the floor of the kitchenette,
and sweeps his wife off her feet.
She scrambles up angrily,
announces they are leaving, now,
and goes downstairs to pack a bag.

He stares, glum, at the damage done,
and notices the sky has turned purple
where a gap in the clouds has formed.
A shaft of violet light shoots through,
and lands on his dining room carpet.

Inside it Good and Evil grapple,
translucent and opaque
in shimmering spandex tights,
Evil in lavender holding the edge,
Good struggling beneath in powder blue,
a fight ineffectual and farcical,
as if a homo-erotic fake masquerade.
Then an angry deep Voice booms,
"I am the one and only God!"
The light ray fades and goes out,
and the perpetual combatants slowly vanish,
but their impressions in the carpet
still wriggle after they're gone.

He is scared witless, and runs down the stairs,
hand to mouth to keep from screaming,
but when he tries to relate to his wife his vision,
she turns to him blankly, clutching her purse.
Below them, the covered carport
high and still dry, is a barren island,
but their car is gone, perhaps the captive
of an early looter getting a leg up
on his rivals, and the beach road
and much of the island is six feet under
in roiling sea water.

All he can do is take his wife inside,
hold her on the stairwell, and wait.

A Big Grill Now

It's cold out here now, man,
the silver things feel cold in my hands,
from the elephants' clasped grey trunks
all the way down to the two Thai lambs.

One hole salt, two holes pepper,
sergeants still stroll on the sands,
birds fly high in a pristine sky;
wasn't that Something grand?

The jagged dagger stabbing me
since Jackie cried in '63,
but ma Michelle knows just who's sane,
O.B. beer for Third World brains;
the gore inside me frozen,
stuck on green and owed one.

Mek We Dweet still makes me sing;
I've been singing solo so long,
and still You Won't See Me.

Eighteen Haiku of Arizona

Valley of the Sun
baseball tourney to be played
five games in five days

catch the Painted Rocks
boulders piled like God's own dung
Native petroglyphs

up early today
breeze gives me a warm greeting
"one hundred degrees"

Verde River Days
folks fish in the green lagoon
meet Smokey the Bear

"Population: strange"
high times in Jerome today
mountain Vieux Carre

manager is late
Diablo Stadium dark
spooks us in some way

four a.m. sounds of
interstate jackhammer bolts
not my job, thank God

curandero guide
Boyce Thompson Arboretum
we hike the high trail

hitless in two games
wooden bat is not to blame
stray gray cat knows so

Gila County ride
such incredible vistas
I can see for miles

Besh-ba-Gowah site
archaeology in Globe
climb staven ladders

antique mall again
no, no shot glasses this time
hard back book of John

Celebrate two hits?
I don't really give two shits
lost the game again

black hawks gliding low
scouting saguaro brush hills
sagely seeking prey

copper mine slag piles
transformations of nature
pennies for your thoughts

La Casita meal
comida Mexicana
green chiles con meats

one more guided tour
Colossal Cave Mountain Park
not so claustro, me

What about baseball?
lost four games in five days
nothing left to say

Who Is It this Time

He awakes just past one
to the drone of Hummers
coming up the block.

The sounds stop as he rises
and slips on his robe;
he tip-toes in socks
up to the front room
to peek out the window.

The vanguard is already
across his whole yard,
their squad leader passes
before him. He cannot discern
from garb or insignia
their branch of service.

He hastens to bed
to warn his wife; the lights
shine through the blinds
all around them. She starts
in attempted remonstration;
he squeezes her hip to silence her.
Her body stiffens as they listen
to the murmur of commands
just outside.

He wonders if he is truly a target,
as he has committed no sins, save
a tin of forbidden herb
he keeps in a drawer.

He doesn't know if or when
they'll burst in, for
in the new order,
warrants are the stuff
of historians.

Fading Flower

Laos Rose,
far from home,
unaccustomed to the cold,
now half-frozen,
growing old,
stands alone.

Laos Rose,
put outside,
sad emotions
she can't hide,
poignant in her
disappointment,
loss of pride.

Laos Rose,
blouse rain-soaked,
sagging bust,
skirt in tatters,
spine exposed,
skin and bones,
but still matters.

Chain Reaction

Cruising down the highway to your beach-side destination
as you try to take a little Labor Day vacation,

I-10 traffic slowing, and you really don't know why,
and then, dead ahead, you see a fireball in the sky;

Just up on the highway, and a tad beyond your vision,
it seems there's little doubt there's been a multi-car collision,

so you put your brakes on, bring your car to a quick stop,
and pull over to the shoulder to wait for the cops;

there are people running from the crash site, and they scream,
and you have to wonder what it is that they've just seen.

Several sirens wailing, as there is help on the way,
one fool sits there blindly, must be texting still in Braille.

There's a part of you that wants to go up there and help,
but another part says better take care of yourself;

Police squad cars, fire engines, ambulances come,
then a second fireball is telling you to run,

and your wife is begging you to get her out harm's way,
so you cross the median, head back to Gautier;

try to get through Pascagoula on old 98,
condo check-in starts at two, and you're already late;

turn on AM radio to get news of the wreck,
but the words you hear are making you feel kind of sick;

none of those involved are now expected to survive,
five are dead already, more than one of them a child;

Your wife says it's a tragedy, her look one of dismay,
but you can only nod, as it is the American way.

Biting My Tongue

A slip of the tongue,
and I bite it;
it shreds like an old tire,
like a chondromalacic medial meniscus
on crystal methedrine.

I spit out a chunk
on the sidewalk,
it lies gleaming,
visceral but dead,
a pickled pig lip
fled its plastic bag,
a pink snail lost its shell.

There is no bleeding,
no pain, pieces breaking
off and ejected methodically,
until no tongue is left
but a nub.

Then it occurs to me:
I may have just muted myself;
perhaps a Freudian slip,
purposely inflicted as a way
to escape my prolonged occupation
based on verbal recitation,
while a poet only really needs,
despite the shouts
of the spoken word crowd,
his pen and something
to write on;
but I also realize
as long as I have
a bit left to grip,
some brain will devise

a blue tooth to fit
my last molar,
and standing at the bar
is where I will stay,
a mannequin making waves.

Generations

I leave my wife and kids
on the beach to play,
and plod my way
through the late morning sun
up to the rental house.
Out on the back deck,
my father lies napping,
sprawled cat-like on his side
on a padded bench,
taking a break from life
with his third wife,
his tenure nearly completed,
and looking ahead to full-
pay retirement, a reward
from the Gret Stet for
thirty years' service to the
Ole War Skule.

I creep across the deck lightly,
as my foot falls always heavy,
a source of many complaints
over the years.
I find myself approaching my recumbent elder,
and I kneel before him,
my face just inches from his,
to make a long uninterrupted
examination of my progenitor.

I reflect on the lines and curves
of his countenance, mine much like his
in many ways, the nose aquiline
with a bump between the eyes,
the legacy of his Germanic mother,
and I realize that at that moment
that we had never been so close.

He had fulfilled his familial duties
in good humor and with cheer,
but there was ever a distance between us;
he was always one step ahead,
his slight unintentional aloofness
a quirk of personality of which
I have been accused;
but I was convinced this day
that I am truly my father's son,
and the similitude has proven itself
time and time again
as the intervening decades
have sped steadily by,
but I am still waiting
for a son from one
of my sons.

Talking Head

The severed head of Saveed,
tossed with detachment from the carriage window,
comes to rest at the crest of the cliffs.
Eyes wide and bulging,
the gagged mouth moving,
the head shouts muffled curses of outrage.
The rocking of jaws starts the head again rolling,
down the downslope and off the precipice;
it hurtles downward two hundred feet
and splashes into the Ulinary below,
where it starts to bob in black wavelets
as bathers gather to see what it is.

Hamir sits in the carriage and hopes
that the fall or the dunking
has finally silenced the evil oracle,
but he has no time to find out.
He ties up his bomb-laden tunic
and turns to the horses,
for he has a body
to dispose of.

Inevitable

If you stand by chance beneath
a red oak of November,
you will soon encounter there
a patter of solid rain,
a sprinkle of ripe fruit falling,
hitting branches and leaves,
and landing on the ground
all around your waiting feet.

The sound's gentle and fleeting,
elusively familiar,
as one drop and another,
peculiar and at random,
slide down through the foliage
to rest in the dirt below.
You're lulled to placid stupor,
fully aware, if you're there long,
that you will be hit in the head,
eventually and inevitably,
but it doesn't really matter.

The acorns sit politely,
doffing their little caps,
a silent, subtle reminder that
the meal for morning's biscuits
lies just within their skins.

Los Mixtos

He sinks in his car seat,
low, below the window,
and hears his *jefito* complain,

a plea to the police
that they must believe him,
no one in his gang is to blame.

To beat a *chiquita*
is too far beneath them,
an act that would demean their name,

but both cops are seething,
the girl is still bleeding,
despite their attempts at first aid.

The voice of Jefito,
both Asian and native,
has such a strange sound under strain

that inside the car,
he must mask a harsh laugh,
but it's his skin that's under her nails.

He hears a cop say
that the girl is awakening,
and he knows he cannot stay;

so despite direct orders,
he will cross the border,
and ditch the jalopy today.

He pulls away slowly,
and in the side mirror,
the face of Jefito is grieved.

He pulls out the parking lot
onto the highway,
and breathes a small sigh of relief.

He soon leaves the highway
to drive the hill skyline,
the pink sunrise makes him feel free;

and as he ascends,
he vows to make amends
once he gets out this hostile country;

but then on the hill climb,
his freedom is short-lived,
he hears the car's engine failing;

the oil pan is leaking,
the thermostat breaking,
a cloud of white steam is rising.

He pulls to the side,
as his ride is now over,
and wishes that he had a drink,

and there by the roadway,
he spies some ripe maguey,
a potion to life on the brink.

He cuts down some stalks
as he starts on his long walk,
an ocean of nerve is his need;

so he sucks the sweet sap
as he makes the trip back
to his rote volunteered slavery,

and soon he will serve
a term that he deserves,
as Jefito determines his fate,

for down in the valley
and deep in the barrio,
he knows Quang Cuello awaits.

Keeping up with the Birds

I stand alone between the buildings,
underneath the overhang,
a lonely smoke break in the shade,
as I'm so frazzled on this day;
I'm light-headed, with dizziness,
and very likely hypotensive;
I'm in need of sustenance,
and can't keep up morale pretenses.

Sparrows are confounding me
with all-around activity,
while one pecks slowly at the pavement,
and then quickly flies away,
another grabs a dried-up clover
to nest in a tall crepe myrtle,
a third flies by my thinning skull
and knows which wire's hot and live;
all in flux, none in a hurry,
doing just what they desire,
and as my mind's eye goes blurry,
but one clear thought occurs to me:
the sparrows that I think I see
must surely number more than three;

and now another has flown down
onto the same spot on the ground,
so furiously does it peck,
that I go over just to check,
and on the concrete, in a crack,
I find a gold clasp marked 12 K,
and right next to it, spread around,
a score or more tiny gold flakes.

I pick them all up carefully,
and fold them in my handkerchief,
as someone's sad calamity

becomes a good fortune for me;
and I'm consoled in finding gold,
so as we reach these final words,
there's one thought I can take from this:
 we all can learn some things from birds.

Gored

Come to in Recovery,
and the wall clock lets me see,
black marks on a pale white face,
just how long was surgery.
Something in me had gone wrong,
and it was not just in a dream;
now my belly's cut and reamed.
My hands explore, and try to trace
the thick pad taped to my navel,
one which I cannot displace,
lest my tightened guts might travel.
Past the blue-gray curtain drawn,
the old surgeon is slowly speaking,
his words certain, warm, and calm,
but my poor head's in such a state
that my glazed brain just can't explain them,
so I find them little balm.

In the next few passing days,
spent within a codeine haze,
my pitiful pain medication
makes a miserable situation,
that all-too-common complication
known by all as constipation.
Now I'm twice-gored, and stuck fast
between the two horns of dilemma,
bound tight, tied up in two places,
pissing, moaning, making faces.
I must now go it alone,
or risk more sickness in not going;
G.I. Blues have me deployed,
so I surrender to the Void.

Less than seven short days out,
I have proven, without doubt,
that manliness is not my game
when it comes to bearing pain;
if I'd required a C-section,
I'd be childless by selection;
and if this was an election,
my recount would beg the question.

A Post-Mortem Regression Digression

I wanted to see my mother
on Mother's Day,
but I couldn't,
because she died
nine years ago
last November.

I wanted to visit her grave,
but I couldn't,
because she wanted
to be cremated,
and she was.

I remember when
we bought her urn.
I picked it out.
It was turquoise blue
and pewter,
and had an Indian
motif, dot
not tomahawk.

I picked up her urn and ashes
from the crematorium.
I had to look inside.
Grinning up at me
was her stent
sitting on a bed
of white-gray ash,
a plastic prophylactic living
past the immolation
of its recipient human.
Then I couldn't get the lid back on
fast enough.

I could've visited the urn.
It sits on my sister's book shelf.
A little of the ashes are left.
I asked my sister to save some.

I wrote my first poems
for my mother.
They were rhymes
about boys with toys,
girls with curls,
dogs and cats,
and baseball bats.
I'd color them to give
to her on days
like Mother's Day.

I can't give my mother any more poems,
so I gave one to my wife
this Mother's Day.
I would have colored it,
but I couldn't find the crayons.
Our kids are grown-ups now,
and their rooms don't look the same..

My mother's ashes
were sent down the river,
at her request,
to rest in the Gulf.
I guess you could venture
that she sleeps with the fishes,

but don't.

Nature, Friends, Is Boring

The sky dances gaily
in blue tongues of flame
atop the white chop
of the rough lake waters.

The stealthy rat scuttles
along the base of the batture,
trying to sneak past
the unwary duck mother
to snatch one of her eggs.

The cottonmouth swims, patient,
beneath the wood deck,
hoping the crippled duckling
will make a fatal misstep
and topple in,

and the blasted red cork,
alone, forever bobbing,
stubbornly refuses
to go under.

The Key

My wife has left me,
I am bereft, an empty basket.
I spend my day in non-stop sobs,
and piteous screams when I throw
and break things.
My sisters have come,
but cannot console me.

My wife has taken up
with an old college classmate,
a widower doctor
from Da Nang.
I knew some day
this would happen.

My sisters walk me down
a dark corridor,
where my predictable lament
is for our dead mom.
We pass a wooden table,
on it a lidded brass jar
that starts to shake.

"Mom? Mom?" I query, and
a thin mist seeps from the jar,
forming a cloud.
Inside is an adobe house with three windows,
in them the faces of our mom
and two cartoon pets; all are smiling.
That's my mother in heaven,
she can't help me.

The jar erupts, the lid flies,
a pale plume rising,
and a small white genie appears.
He marvels at the realness
of his surroundings,
and I clutch his chalky hand,
opaque yet solid.

My older sister beseeches him;
he bids me to attend, and murmurs:
"This is the Key." A screen glows
before my eyes, but in brown and orange,
with medieval text
about Kodiak bears.

I cry out my protest,
but my little sister wants to read it,
she saw it on Discovery.
I claw the screen aside,
but the genie is gone, and I moan,
resigned.

Now I see my life on the screen,
a dated black-and-white
sign-off signal from an old local station,
cursed pelican in perpetual leer.
My future is now
is my past.

Respite

You'll find unburied
some small sets of bones
by the banks of the river's
dark bar pit.

Misères abandoned there
rendered to stone,
but will grow
in the darkness of closets.

Griots tell stories
of poor girls' lost souls,
babies still-born, and those
that could cause it.

Cold-eyed grey vultures
are circling low,
as they wait
for the next bank deposit.

Deep in the Bunker

As they enter the last hallway,
word is passed that the point
of final attack has been changed.
Hamir is at once apprehensive;
perhaps something is amiss.
They escort their fake prisoners,
all armed under their loose jail suits,
past the back wall, which is tapped
by the traitor sitwa to indicate where
the Sajan sits listening to a Jacceba
quartet playing their ragas.

They turn the final corner,
and Hamir sees more Fatwehs
painted into the mural,
waiting to spring back into
three dimensions on the signal
to aid the break and start
the conflagration.
Hamir thinks he catches the eye
of one still commissar.
They pass the supply room
and their beady-eyed mole
winks surreptitiously, showing
he and his men are ready.

All halt. The knave sitwa hands
their papers to the Sitwa Prima
at the gates; they discuss orders
in clipped, precise Jacceba.
The Prima, now irritated
because their arrival has caused him
to miss most of the first ragas,
pushes by so close to Hamir
that their shoulders brush.

Hamir's vision starts to swirl,
and he is seized by an irresistible urge
to detonate his explosives
now.

The Academician

He stands erect in the rented room,
equipment inspected and protected,
tonight's whore bent over a chair,
adorned by red lingerie worn
at his request.

"Don't look at me," he murmurs,
but makes sure he can see
both his face and hers
in the bathroom mirror
beyond the open door.

"Let me love you," he implores,
but the four-letter word
he tries so to croon
gets stuck in his craw
and curdles to a gurgle.

Her face is impatient,
time is used, useless, wasting;
he arms himself until ready.

High in the mount,
his moon face reddens;
he is caught in the act.
Now he sees everything:
Hobbes and Goethe were both correct
past any question;
he watches two pigs sweating
in full rut.

John Lambremont Sr.

Posted—No Entry

Your notes by the door
all had plenty of stick-em,
but would not support
a dead dog.

Your sharpie bled through,
red ink on the white plaster,
your handwriting now
on the wall.

My bloody hand's caught,
wrist deep into the sheetrock,
long after the punching
is done.

My fingers extend,
all thin, broken, and feeble,
still reaching for your
cheating heart.

Your message was clear,
you were dearly departed;
we're much more than
mere walls apart,

but here we will stay,
both entrapped and uncharted,
until your worms turn loose
my arm.

The Survivor State

We survived Kennedy
We survived Hilda
We survived Betsy
We survived King
We survived Johnson
We survived Camille
We survived Saigon
and we survived the Rings.

We survived Agnew
We survived Nixon
We survived Kruschev
We survived disco
We survived Uncle Ho
We survived the Chairman
and we survived the Corleones.

We survived the Carter years
We survived the fatted Shah
We survived poor John-John Lennon
We survived the Mardi Gras
We survived the ayatollahs
We survived the Gipper's claw
and we survived the Berlin Wall.

We survived the stupid economy
We survived the Andrew storm
We survived the burning Bush
We survived the first Gulf War
We survived the Billaristas
We survived impeachment hearings
and we survived the viral swarms.

We survived the Y2k
We survived the nine one one
We survived the big dick chaining
We survived the Bushes' son
We survived the bitch Katrina
We survived her sister Rita
and we survived the BP pee.

Sunset on False River

There's just one catfish in the cooler,
but what a fine afternoon it's been,
partly cloudy, warm and breezy,
a leavened slice of early May
snuck from a February freezer.

To the west, a weary sun slips
sullen into sheets of gray,
taking his leave with a angry wink,
a warning of what is to come.
The low bed starts to glow, and turns
into a crouching purple dragon, fire flowing
from between the scales of its skin,
then the sun reaches rest and explodes,
sending a crescendo of vivid colors,
pinks and purples, orange, reds and blues,
to splash against the walls and ceiling.

To the east, the baby moon peeks
from beneath her fluffed white blankets,
then lifts her head to look around
her early evening room of blue.
She sits up in bed to catch my eye,
her pretty round face is full of smiles,
as she is the river's daughter,
and reflects down on her mother,
for she knows she is golden ascending.

"Dear God, what glories have you set
before my non-believing eyes;
a hot, magnificent sun in set,
and a beautiful, warm moon-rise."

After the Rig Collapse

All the tugboats and crew boats,
Coast Guard cutters and 'copters,
and commercial fishers and shrimpers
rush to The Pickets to pick up survivors
from the waters. The blow-out preventers
have, thankfully, held, and there was
no explosion or oil spill this time,
so the death toll is expected
to be low.

Your wife is a Red Cross volunteer,
and has left for the mainland
to help at the aid station.
A few minutes after she's left,
you stand on the back beach,
taking in the gray skies and stiff winds,
when the high-rise bay bridge
begins to tremble slightly, then gives in,
collapsing in the middle, pillars falling
like dominoes toward both shores,
the victims of sub-grade cement,
bid-rigging, and political rookery,
and you don't know whether or not
your wife has made it across alive.

In a panic, you try to iPhone her,
but there is no answer, just ringing,
and the local news app has only
rig collapse and "the new Katrina"
screaming across the Gulf.
All residents of the island
are advised to evacuate now,
before the island goes under,
via the bay bridge.

A Category 4

1.

I never fathomed Galveston,
nor Isle Derniere,
for animals can tell when you
when a hurricane is near;

the Gulf's breath is all over you,
fetid, menacing;
the dogs start getting nervous,
and the birds no longer sing;

and then there's no more speculation
when the clouds reach circular circulation.

2.

Hey, Mister, that's me inside the plywood;
I won't have old man wing-tips on my forehead,
so if You're going to kill me, kill me now.
You know my branches are split already,
and my Spirit has long since sailed,
so I dare You to try it again.

3.

The silent trees scream, tortured;
their helpless limbs flail, whipped.
The dogs are quiet now,
as only the wind howls.
I peek out from the back door
as the storm peaks in our quarter;
and then in a ghastly tomb of sound,
the cracking barrel reports, I watch
as the sturdier oak goes down,

a clumsy fall to the hedgerow,
and a sprawl down to the ground.
I stand there, dumb, and wonder
how much life can yet remain
for its skinny surviving brother.

4.

There's no reward in heavy labor;
it can't restore or rehabilitate,
unless your reward's to restore your yard
to its pre-storm semi-unkempt state;

with all the downed trees in your way,
and more rain clouds on the horizon,
but for no sun is what you pray;

and now you toil like a foot soldier,
foliage dragging in your wake,
and echoes meddle with your power:
now you are their anguished slave.

The Woodman

The first shot comes without a warning,
splintering his wood picket;
he drops his hatchet-axe and runs,
like a rabbit through the thicket,
to the safety of the woods
where life is good, and guns are wicked.

Three black suits are in pursuit,
as slugs thud into trunks nearby;
he finds the special tree of entry,
throwing himself headlong at it;
it absorbs his very being,
and he climbs inside to hide.

He transfers to an oak adjoining,
and slides through into its core;
he sees one of the black suits pointing
a small box not seen before,
and then he knows he's being detected
and a flight for life's in store;

so he is chased from tree to tree,
evading through connecting leaves,
but his pursuers he can't escape,
and soon his airways start to wheeze;
he seeks some shelter in a cabin,
crouched inside a ceiling eave.

Then two black suits enter the cabin,
holding flare guns and carbines,
one scans four unvarnished walls,
as he looks for the refugee,
the third stands next to the rear entry,
waiting for their prey to flee.

The Woodman crouches in his rafter,
praying for a gentle breeze
to bring a close tree into contact,
so that he can make his leave;
he tries to stop his shoulders' heaving,
for he knows that wood can breathe.

Disharmonious Harmony

And so it came to pass,
an edict from the High Prefecture, proclaiming
that music for the multitudes
was just far too important
to be left to the professionals
and the hacks, and
decreeing that henceforth
in every borough, hamlet, and burg,
every man and woman,
save the truly afflicted
and the village idiots,
and every boy and girl
of the age of discernment
or older, would be required
to play an instrument
and contribute to the vocals,
and that the combined efforts of all
would become the new music,
to be played exclusively
throughout the state.

And so to each place
a single song was sent,
mostly old show tunes
of the last Century,
and the people were herded,
oft-times by force,
into recording studios,
and few dared to refuse,
as the penalties for avoidance
were severe.

The results were abominable,
unrecognizable and unlistenable,
as all the musicians, conductors,
and music scholars fled

across the mountain gap
to neighboring Intelligentsia,
but the High Prefects extolled
the new music as shining
samples of patriotism,
and had it played
on every corner in every town;
and, within a few months' time,
street crimes had dropped off
by more than half,
and the slender murder rate
went down
to zero.

Ask if You Will

How far back
do you want to see?
And what stranger tales
do you believe there to be?

I've laid bare to you but a part of my soul,
a sour-sop soda and an old jelly roll,
bound, tied, and twisted at age twenty-three,
a subsistent existence, now pushing sixty.

I never confessed for my sins or disease,
but I sometimes still ended up
on my knees.

The Future Home of the Tabernacle of God

It was still early dusk when I drove into Grayson.
My eye was distracted and drawn
by a sign and the tract that lay beyond it.
The plot was thin, but ran deep,
ringed on three sides by pine forest and yaupon.
The land had been cleared but once, long ago,
and the scrub and brush rose as high as a camel's eye,
unmowed for so long, so long,
that how long, God himself might only know.

In the gray twilight, I noted an owl's nest
high up in a tree, while brown skippers danced turns
with summer flowers, birds flew to and fro,
squirrels searched for pine nuts amongst the needles,
and fireflies flashed green lights of approval,
but mourning crickets filled my ears
with ubiquitous and sad lamenting.

The sign was dilapidated,
the paint peeling and faded,
and was falling apart in part.
I wondered what kind of tabernacle
could be spread on a sliver so slender,
and whether the funds had run out,
or perhaps the pastor's flock had bolted.
I surmised that this space, a dream first deferred
and then abandoned, would never be a house of God,
but then I grinned to no one,
and said silently to myself,
"It is already; it already is."

A Reincarnation

Two potted palms straddle our driveway,
given to us by a nephew on the move,
remnants from the shotgun house
in old Beauregard Town downtown
where my wife's people lived before
the neighborhood was overrun
by law offices, small businesses,
and Court support.

Planted a score ago by my wife's father,
they have flourished on Tom's back patio;
we retrieve them and carry them back upriver
eighty miles to our suburban abode,
and call them by the names
our children gave their maternal grandparents,
Grandpa and Grandma, and over years,
the palms take the paths
of their namesakes.

Grandpa is tall, a seeker of light;
he thrusts himself toward the sun,
leaning over the rim of his urn,
guiding his surrounding children,
seeming by appearance to live eternally,
sharp of mind and strong of will,
but his legs have become weakened,
and he sometimes topples over
when storms bring forth high winds.

Grandma is diminutive and quiet,
never moving, all growth behind her,
and almost before we know it,
she sickens with infestatious disease,
lingers briefly, and succumbs,
and we mourn her, wishing
we had done more.

We thought her gone forever,
but this spring she re-emerged,
rising slowly in the warming sun,
her grandchildren at her feet,
tugging at her apron for favor.
She leans slightly toward Grandpa,
and softly whispers his name
onto the passing breezes.

Grandpa looks back over his shoulder,
extends one long-sleeved arm,
and beckons her to his side.

620 Conti Street

We never asked which one was Castillo,
whether the squat matron that ran the floor,
the old man that sat at the corner table library,
or the burly *hombrote* negro that would come out
from the kitchen in back to glower,
or none of them.

On our first visit, I extolled the *sopa* on the menu
to my wife, chicken stock with shrimp, crab, tomatoes,
onions, and cilantro swimming in it,
a homemade recipe I'd not tasted
since my college trips to Puebla,
similar in taste to the shrimp and crab ball soup
my wife's people concocted
on the Far East side of the Pacific rim.
"No soup today," the woman said.

I asked her about the *guacamole de casa*
featured on the menu.
"No guacamole today," she said.

I asked her about the *puerco con salsa verde*,
whether the sauce was tomatillo-based.
"No green sauce today," she said.
"Red sauce."

So we ordered the *flautas de pollo*,
sin guacamole, of course,
and the *puerco con salsa roja*,
and found the *comida*,
accompanied by *arroz y frijoles*,
tasty, filling, inexpensive,
and *muy auténica*,
so we soon became regulars.

Quickly, we came to realize
that this café was built on a broken business model,
as disorganization, disarray, and indifference
were its prime movers and motivators.
Each visit, we were greeted by the Mona Lisa
half-smile of the matron, her intonation
of no soup, no guacamole, no black sauce
her daily mantra. She would not hesitate
to switch the door sign from *"abierta"* to *"cerrada"*
any time she seated more than three tables,
usually in response to an angry glare
from the surly cook,
and she never changed expressions when she corrected
my poor attempts at Spanish;

but the food was good, served hot
and made with fresh ingredients.
The red sauce was savory and fiery,
and the *salsa verde*, full of tomatillo and garlic,
graced the best *enchiladas Suizas* I've ever had,
but a part of our fascination
was the complete lack of care as to customer satisfaction
or profit, as the place was usually empty,
and the woman reveled in turning diners away.

The old man, for all we knew, a latter-day Neruda,
Castaneda, or Marquez, never spoke to us
or acknowledged our presence,
reading or writing quietly at his corner table
surrounded by books, papers, and book shelves
filled to the brim.
He smoked a careful Meerschaum,
and called the woman over occasionally
for a whispered communiqué.

We never found out if he was her
husband, or father, or uncle,
or no relation at all.

We grew resigned to never tasting
the soup or the guacamole,
and never having available the red sauce and
the green sauce on the same day,
and our curiosity was piqued even further
the day the matron explained the eternal absence
of the *salsa negro*. The black sauce,
she related, was made in the Yucatan,
near Merida, and formed into large bricks,
requiring the old man to go there personally
to purchase and bring back the product.
The old man, she confided somewhat scornfully,
was getting too old and creaky to make the trip,
and had resisted it successfully for some time.

By then we were starting to wonder
if the restaurant was on the up-and-up,
or was a front for some nefarious enterprise.
Our suspicions were exacerbated by our trips
to the unisex bathroom, narrow and long,
where a single bald light bulb revealed shelves
on every wall full of a thousand or more rolls
of *papel de baño*, all white (of course),
more toilet paper than customers or staff
could ever use in *cien años*.
They seemed to plead silently for our attention,
as if figuring them out
was the key to all understanding.

ACKNOWLEGEMENTS

"The Day Our Home Exploded" appeared previously in *Used Gravitrons*

"Suburb in Rondo" appeared previously in *A Hudson View*

"Delta Deep Freeze appeared previously in *Broken Circles* by Cave Moon Press

"Food Fight" appeared previously in Local Gems Poetry Press' *Rhyme and Punishment* anthology

"I, Drunkie" and "The Key" appeared previously in *ISFN Anthology #1*

"Pachuco y Juanito" appeared previously in *Caper Literary Journal*

"Earth Invader" appeared previously in *Breadcrumb Sins*

"Dummy" appeared previously in *The Minetta Review*

"A Big Loss" appeared previously in *The Glass Coin*

"Funereal" appeared previously in *Poetry Quarterly*

"The Lay Of The Land" appeared previously in *The Stray Branch*

"Skull Session" appeared previously in *Greensilk Journal*

"Eighteen Haiku of Arizona" appeared previously in *Bear Creek Haiku*

"The Survivor State" appeared previously in *Poets for Living Waters*

"Ulinary Uprising," "In The Aftermath," and "The Jacceba Usurper" appeared previously in *Extraterrestrial Life* by Nazer Look

"The Woods Grow Silent" appeared previously in *The Gulf Stream: Poems of the Gulf South* anthology by Snake-Nation Press

"Posted-No Entry" appeared previously in the *Shattered* anthology by Kind Of A Hurricane Press

"Sunset On False River" appeared previously in the *Long River Run* anthology by the Connecticut Poetry Society

"Disharmonious Harmony" appeared previously in *Pacific Review*

www.ingramcontent.com/pod-product-compliance
Lightning Source LLC
Chambersburg PA
CBHW021003090426
42738CB00007B/639